PREPARING FOR
CONFESSION

L. Joseph Letendre

ANCIENT FAITH PUBLISHING
CHESTERTON, INDIANA

Published by:
    Ancient Faith Publishing
    A Division of Ancient Faith Ministries
    1050 Broadway, Suite 6
    Chesterton, IN 46304

All Old Testament quotations, unless otherwise identified, are from the
Orthodox Study Bible, © 2008 by St. Athanasius Academy of Orthodox
Theology (published by Thomas Nelson, Inc., Nashville, Tennessee)
and are used by permission. New Testament quotations are from the
New King James Version of the Bible, © 1982 by Thomas Nelson, Inc.,
and are used by permission.

ISBN: 978-1-955890-28-1

Cover image: *Confession* by Sergey Efoshkin, oil on canvas, 1994.
With gratitude to the artist.

Contents

Foreword

It is instructive to observe that the command to repent, when it appears in the Bible, is sometimes expressed in what grammarians call "the present tense imperative"; in this case, the verb *repent* bears the sense of "repent again," even "keep on repenting." That is to say, the command *repent* is not always directed to those who have yet to do so (Acts 2:38; 3:19) but also to those who may need to do it again (Matt. 3:2; 4:17).

When they sin (*when*, not *if*), Christian believers also need to repent. A Christian can never say of repentance, "Ah, yes, I've already done that. Now let's do something else, maybe something new and exciting."

The example of St. Peter amply demonstrates this need for renewed repentance in the Church. Even after his confession of Jesus as Son of God (Matt. 16:16), Peter fell so grievously as to deny even knowing him (26:69–75). Nonetheless, Peter was not cut adrift from divine grace and the communion of the Church. He was required to repent again, perhaps even more seriously than the first time.

Moreover, Peter made sure the whole Church would know about this need for renewed repentance; this is why his story is told in all four Gospels. Peter made no secret of his sin so that all of us would know that the path to repentance is *always* open.

And here we come to an important feature of repeated

repentance: it is not just a private affair. No matter how "private" the circumstances in which they are committed, all sins after Baptism are offenses, not only against God but also against the holiness and communion of the Church. For this reason, purely private repentance is not enough. Peter himself, quoting the Book of Leviticus, emphasizes the ongoing imperative of holiness within the Church: "Be holy, for I am holy" (1 Pet. 1:16; Lev. 11:44–45, 19:2, 20:7).

The confession of sins involves the Church for the same reason Baptism involves the Church. Both rites are sacramental actions *of the Church*. In the case of our first repentance, it is the Church that baptizes; it is also the Church, acting through her presbyteral ministry, that absolves the again-repentant Christian. Indeed, one of the earliest names of Confession was "second repentance."[1]

And because Confession pertains to the holiness of the Christian life, it gradually became, over the course of history, the pastoral setting for spiritual direction and counsel. All serious Christians need guidance. No believer is ever simply on his own. This sacrament represents the Church's reluctance to let any of her children become lost and confused in their own spiritual darkness. We believers belong to Noah's Ark, not some private yachting club.

For this reason, the Father Confessor is not just a private counselor. Even as he tailors his guidance to the specific needs of each soul, he must never forget that he speaks for and with the authority of the Church. The priest should remind himself that his counsel to the penitent is an extension of his ministry in the pulpit; when he listens to the sins of fallen Christians, he is especially charged to proclaim the Gospel once again, the "good news" of mercy and salvation.

Likewise, the priest is never to stand in judgment over the

---

1 This expression, from third-century Latin Africa, is the title of Bernhard Poschmann's magisterial study of Confession, *Paenitentia Secunda: Die kirchliche Busse im ältesten Christentum bis Cyprian und Origenes* (Bonn, 1940).

struggling, repentant soul. He acts as a counselor and intercessor—*parakletos*—not a judge. His words must be directed to hope, not discouragement.

On the part of the repentant sinner, on the other hand, this *penitentia secunda* must not become routine and haphazard. If the act of confessing one's sins to the forgiving Church is taken seriously, the penitent sinner should prepare his heart and mind for this solemn act. He has an obligation to take stock of his conscience because Confession is integral to his duty to strive for holiness. Confession is not magic, nor is the absolution some sort of incantation. The responsibility to repent is grave and not to be taken lightly.

Consequently, we are once again indebted to Joseph Letendre for this new edition of his guide to the discipline of Confession. Do not be deceived by the relative brevity of this book. It is an important work that addresses a concrete pastoral need. I am honored to recommend it.

Indeed, let me render a couple of suggestions to my fellow priests. First, make sure you place a free copy of this book in the hand of every new adult convert to the Orthodox Church; make sure everyone understands the purpose of this book and its contents. Second, recommend this book within the setting of the sacrament itself, especially in those cases where a penitent seems to require specific instruction on the subject.

Finally, let me commend the wisdom of Ancient Faith Publishing in making sure Joseph Letendre's work remains available in the Church.

Fr. Patrick Henry Reardon
All Saints Orthodox Church, Chicago, Illinois

Understanding Sin

In every sacrament, there is an act of offering. In the Eucharist, we offer bread and wine; in Baptism and Chrismation and at Ordinations, we offer ourselves or our children; in Marriage, we offer the relationship that has flowered between two people; and in anointing, we offer human sickness and suffering. In the Sacrament of Reconciliation—Confession—it is our own sinfulness that we bring as an offering.

When we stand before the icons with the priest beside us, what should we say? What sins must we confess? What do we offer? And, perhaps most importantly, how do we discover what we should say? These are the questions I will try to answer here.

WHAT IS SIN?

Sin Is Not Just Breaking the Ten Commandments

We often think of Confession as a presentation of a "shopping list" that indicates the ways we've broken the Ten Commandments. But this approach can lead to confusion. I haven't robbed any banks or murdered anyone, I'm faithful to my spouse, and so far, I've resisted the temptation to sacrifice my children to idols. Why then does the priest insist I am a sinner? And why does the Church require that I go to Confession when I haven't done anything?

The painful truth is that it's possible to keep all the Commandments and yet still be in sin. The Ten Commandments largely focus on what we should not do—the famous "Thou shalt nots." God gave them so that He could weave a recently enslaved, nomadic group of people into what today we would call a civil society. These commandments are obvious and, in one form or another, universal. Sooner or later, violations will be publicly noticeable. This is true even in the case of adultery. Adulterers may convince themselves that they are "being discreet," but the damage they inflict on those around them will be felt even if the cause is hidden. And it will not stay hidden forever, as Numbers 32:23 says: "you have sinned against the LORD; and be sure your sin will find you out" (NKJV).

However, there is another category of sin that can easily go unnoticed by ourselves and those around us. Traditionally, these are called "sins of omission"—the things we leave out, the things we neglect. These are the hardest kind of sin to recognize and to repent.

These are also the sins that drew Jesus' harshest criticism of the Pharisees: "For you pay tithe of mint and anise and cummin, and have neglected the weightier *matters* of the law: justice and mercy and faith" (Matt. 23:23). These are the sins for which, in our Lord's Parable of the Last Judgment (also known as the Parable of the Sheep and the Goats), the "goats" are condemned. It is not the wrong things they did but the good they failed to do that leads the Lord to say, "Depart from Me, you cursed, into the everlasting fire prepared for the devil and his angels . . . inasmuch as you did not do *it* to one of the least of these, you did not do *it* to Me" (Matt. 25:41, 45).

Keeping the Ten Commandments is the necessary but insufficient first step. God expects more. He aims to make us more than law-abiding citizens; He wants to make us saints. He commands us to "be holy as I am holy" (Lev. 11, 19, 20; 1 Pet. 1:16) and reminds us that the greatest commandment is to "love the LORD your God with all your heart, with all your soul, and with all your mind" and to "love your neighbor as yourself" (Matt. 22:37, 39). His aim is nothing less than to restore in us his own image and likeness.

Missing the Mark

To understand more clearly what sin is, we must look at the word the New Testament and many of the Fathers use for sin: *hamartia*. This Greek word means "missing the mark." For the writers of the New Testament and those Fathers who wrote in Greek, sin meant being off target, moving in the wrong direction, aiming for the wrong goal. But what goal should we strive for?

Saint Paul writes that we should attain "the measure of the stature of the fullness of Christ" (Eph. 4:13). This is the goal. Like Christ, we must be filled with the Holy Spirit and always do the will of the Father. This means that the measuring stick we use when we confess is not how well or how poorly we are keeping the rules. Nor is it whether we seem better or worse when we compare ourselves to others. The measuring stick is the Person of Jesus of Nazareth. Thus, one definition of sin could be "deliberate unChristlike behavior."[2] We will see later what this means practically for repentance and confessing our sins.

Spiritual Disease

When we do something foolish or make a mistake, we often say, "Well, I'm only human." But human beings by definition are creatures made in the image and likeness of God. Being human is not an excuse for weakness and foolishness; it is a call to holiness. Sin is a failure to live up to our high calling. When we are sinful, we fail to be truly human as God wishes us to be. This means that sin is abnormal in human beings. It is a sickness that distorts the image of God in us.

---

2 Michael Casey, *Sacred Reading* (Liguori, MO: Liguori Publications, 1995), 92.

Some of the specific sins that trouble us may be symptoms of underlying sins the Fathers call passions. For example, we may confess to losing our temper, but the root of this sin may be jealousy or pride. In this medical model of sin and repentance, the priest's task, as we shall see, is to diagnose and prescribe.

PREPARING FOR CONFESSION

A good confession happens before we even leave for church. In Jesus' Parable of the Prodigal Son, when the young man finally comes to his senses, he says, "I will arise and go to my father, and will say to him, 'Father, I have sinned against heaven and before you, and I am no longer worthy to be called your son. Make me like one of your hired servants'" (Luke 15:18–19). Before the son takes one step on the journey back to his father, he rehearses what he will say. In other words, he prepares. We must do the same. A good confession depends on good preparation.

How do we prepare for Confession? First, we must set aside some time to prepare: a half hour, at least. This must be a period of time when we will be free from distractions and interruptions. We should not be shy about asking our family to help protect this time. One of the most loving things husbands and wives can do for each other is to safeguard each other's time and place of prayer. This can mean taking the children out, answering the phone, or turning off the TV.

Preparation should also happen in a place where we will not be disturbed. We can go to our room and close the door. We can sit before our icons. But we must find a place where we can relax and be quiet for the duration of time we have set aside to prepare.

Once we have entered the time and place to prepare for Confession, we must fill it with four things: silence, prayer, reading, and reflection.

Silence and Solitude

We begin simply by placing ourselves in God's presence. We say to Him, "Here I am." We remind ourselves that for the next half hour or so, our time and thoughts will be His and His alone. And we keep silent.

Anyone who has tried this knows what soon happens. We forget about God quickly. We become bored, and then all sorts of thoughts flood our minds. Anger about what someone said or did to us weeks ago comes bubbling to the surface, and we find ourselves fantasizing about what we should have said or done. Last night's TV show, a song we heard on the radio, or a scene from the last movie we saw may play back in our minds. We get fidgety. We remember all the things we've put off for months and feel a sudden urgency to do them right now.

When we realize that our mind has wandered, we should bring our attention back to God through prayer, especially the Jesus Prayer.

Prayer

The single most important thing we can do to prepare for Confession is to pray. Unless the Holy Spirit reveals our sins and sinfulness to us, we will not see them. In prayer, we ask God to show us what He finds displeasing in us, what He wants us to repent of. If we are concerned only with how we're disappointed in ourselves, repentance can become an exercise in self-improvement but not a return to the Father.

We discover our sins not by seeing how evil we are but by seeing how good God is. The more brightly lit a room is, the more clearly we see the dust and cobwebs. In the lives of saints, we often see that the holier they became, the more they realized how sinful they were. In prayer, we can begin to see our sins as clearly as God sees them. Through prayer, we meet our God as the God of forgiveness and mercy, and we see the sinfulness of our anger and judgment of others; we find Him as the generous giver of all good things and are convicted in our greed, jealousy, and material anxiety. We encounter the humble Lord of glory, and we see the foolishness of our pride and conceit; we are embraced by the God who is love and so recognize our selfishness and lust for what they truly are. In the end, we discover that even sins against our neighbor are ultimately sins against God. Like the Psalmist, we can then pray, "Against You only have I sinned / And done evil in Your sight" (Ps. 50:6/51:4).

How should we pray? It is good to begin with the prayers "O Heavenly King" and the Trisagion Prayers. In this way, our prayers are united to the prayers of the entire Church. Then we can use other written prayers from a book, the Jesus Prayer, our own words, or prayers from the Bible. The Psalms are especially good, particularly Psalms 31/32, 37/38, and 50/51, which are psalms of repentance. (These and other psalms are included in the Appendix.)

It is important to pray slowly. Pause after words and phrases so they can sink in and touch the heart. Our prayer should echo the prayer of the Psalmist: "Who will understand his transgressions? / Cleanse me from hidden sins" (Ps. 18:13/19:12).

Reading

Reading helps us to discern errors. In particular, reading can provide the right standard by which we must measure ourselves. This right standard is not the world around us or what we see others doing; we are not good Christians just because we are no worse than other people. Nor does the standard of perfection consist of our own goals and aspirations. As I said above, our standard and measuring stick is the Person of Jesus Christ. It is Christ who tells us, in the midst of a dog-eat-dog world, "blessed are the meek." He is the one who asks us, "Are you the kind of person I am? The person My Father wants you to be?"

For this reason, reading from the Bible is most important. The Sermon on the Mount (Matt. 5–7) and 1 Corinthians 13 are good places to start. By following a rule of daily Scripture readings, we will find other passages we can return to when preparing for Confession. We should write these verses down so they will be conveniently available when we next prepare. In addition, reading from Father Thomas Hopko's booklet *If We Confess Our Sins* or the confession from *The Way of the Pilgrim* can help us to focus and apply the Scripture to our own sins.

The last thing to say about reading is that this is not the time to gather ammunition to use on the Jehovah's Witnesses when they come to the door or the "Pharisee" who sits with us on the parish council. What we read we must apply to ourselves, not to our neighbor.

Reflection

Finally, we must actively take what we gather from our silence, prayer, and reading, and examine ourselves. To do this successfully, we must have an attitude of self-blame or self-accusation. This is a very hard attitude to cultivate. We naturally want to see ourselves in the best light, and we want others to think well of us. Self-accusation goes against our nature. It means refusing to make excuses or compare ourselves with others. It means playing the role of prosecutor instead of defense attorney. Saint Dorotheos of Gaza, a sixth century monk, tells a story that may help us understand.

> There once came to me two brothers who were always [arguing], and the elder was saying about the younger, "I arrange for him to do something and he gets distressed, and so I get distressed, thinking that if he had faith and love towards me he would accept what I tell him with complete confidence." And the younger was saying, ". . . but he does not speak to me with the fear of God, but rather as someone who wants to give orders." Impress on your minds that each blames the other and neither blames himself. . . . What

they really ought to do is just the opposite. The first ought to say: I speak with presumption and therefore God does not give my brother confidence in me. And the other ought to be thinking: My brother gives me commands with humility and love but I am unruly and have no fear of God. . . . Each considers himself right and excuses himself, as I was saying, all the while keeping none of the Commandments yet expecting his neighbor to keep the lot! . . . Ought we not rather to examine ourselves about the Commandments and blame ourselves for not keeping them?[3]

Another thing to remember is that in our actual preparation, these elements—silence, prayer, reading, and reflection—will not follow one after another but will be mixed. Our silence may lead to reading, our reading to prayer or more silence, and so on. The order of these activities is not important: this will vary from person to person and even from confession to confession. What is important is that we include all these ingredients. Let me give some examples of how this might work for you.

We are silent before God and, frankly, bored. We pray, but we cannot pay attention to prayer. This can lead us to reflect on how little we must truly love God, for we find His company so dull. Or perhaps we are distracted from silence and prayer by worry and by anxiety about money. Then we read in the Gospel Jesus' command not to worry about these things (Matt. 6:25–34). We can reflect on our lack of trust in our heavenly Father.

One last note: Make sure to write down these reflections and bring the list to Confession if you think you might forget the sins you need to mention.

---

3 Eric P. Wheeler, trans., *Discourses and Saying by Dorotheos of Gaza* (Kalamazoo, MI: Cistercian Publications, 1977), 144–46.

Scheduling

When and how often should we go to Confession? Depending on the type of confession we want to make, there are two answers: as soon as possible, or regularly.

As soon as possible. Unfortunately, there can be moments in our lives when we commit truly serious sins. The Ten Commandments specifically identify these. Historically, in its penitential discipline, the Church summed them up as murder, adultery, and apostasy: sins that barred us from receiving Communion because the Eucharist would then lead to our judgment and condemnation. Just as a serious injury will send us hurrying for medical care, some sins should send us hurrying for pastoral care.

We should confess promptly anything else we do or fail to do that disturbs us, troubles our conscience, or wrecks our peace of soul. In her worship and prayers, the Church distinguishes between two kinds of sins: voluntary and involuntary. Some have suggested that "of malice or weakness" might be a clearer translation. Sins that are voluntary or of malice—the things we do deliberately even though we know they are wrong—should be quickly confessed. When we feel weighed down by a heavy and torturous burden, it only makes sense to put that burden down as soon as we can.

Regularly. Going to Confession is not usually on the top of anyone's "favorite things about being Orthodox" list. It's something we prefer to avoid and are likely to put off. Thus, it's crucial to establish a set schedule to undertake the preparation described in these pages and to present ourselves and our confession to our priest. Confession is part of our *ascesis*—it takes its place alongside prayer, fasting, sacrifice, and silence in the collection of practices we need in order to follow Christ faithfully and effectively. Because of our reluctance, we must make Confession a regularly scheduled activity, a routine part of our lives.

Fortunately, it's not up to us to devise a schedule. Our parish priest will set a preferred discipline for the parish. In some parishes, this may be on a monthly basis, or at least four times a year—during the Church's fasting seasons. In others, particularly parishes of the Russian tradition, parishioners are asked to confess before each time they take communion. It's also possible that at certain times our priest will ask us to come more often, so that the grace and guidance this sacrament provides may arm and support us during a difficult time in our lives or in our struggle with some habitual failing. All we have to do is follow the schedule and come on time. In the words of our Lord, "Do this and you will live" (Luke 10:28).

Life Prepares Us

So far we have been talking about particular preparation for Confession. But there is also a general sort of preparation. Since the whole of the Christian life is a struggle with sin and temptation and involves an ongoing effort of repentance, all of life can prepare us for Confession.

This is obviously true of the overtly spiritual aspects of our lives: prayer, the liturgy, sermons, spiritual reading, fasting. All these can give us insights into ourselves that we should bring to Christ in Sacramental Confession. But there is more: If we cultivate the attitude of self-accusation, God can use practically anything in our lives to reveal our hidden sins to us.

Pambo, a fourth century desert father, once went into the city of Alexandria. He happened to see a prostitute and began to weep. Those who were with him asked why he wept, and he said, "Two things make me weep: one, the loss of this woman; and the other, that I am not as concerned to please God as she is to please wicked men."[4]

In another example, in the nineteenth century, Macarius,

---

4 Benedicta Ward, trans., *Sayings of the Desert Fathers* (Kalamazoo, MI: Cistercian Publications, 1975), 165.

an elder in the Russian monastery of Optino, once wrote to a correspondent:

> You say your maid annoys and irritates you so much that, in order not to fly into a rage, you have taken to telling her—whenever you feel a paroxysm coming on—that she must not lead you into temptation, after which you hurriedly leave the room. This seems to me a remarkably weak way of combating the root of the evil.
>
> Consider her, in this connection, as being used by God to show you your greatest weakness: this rage which slumbers in you at all times but lies hidden until she, the hand of God, discloses it.[5]

For Pambo and Macarius, God used the prostitute and the maid to lead them to see their sins and to repent more deeply. If we are alert and listen for God, who speaks to us in a gentle whisper (3Kg. 19:11–12), there will be many moments of our lives that God will use to show us where we need to change.

I have said much about preparing for Confession because I am convinced that what we actually say before the priest in Confession is only the tip of the iceberg; it is the fruit of our preparation.

WHAT *NOT* TO SAY

I cannot tell you what you should say in Confession. Prepare, and what you must say will be made clear to you. But I can tell you six things you should not say if you wish to make a good confession.

1. *"I Have No Sins"*

This is very frustrating for a priest to hear. How is he to absolve in Christ the sins of someone who claims not to have any? How

---

5   Iulia de Beausobre, trans., *Russian Letters of Direction by Macarius, Starets of Optino* (Yonkers, NY: St. Vladimir's Seminary Press, 1974), 78.

can he give that person the Body and Blood of Christ "for the remission of sins?" But this situation is even more serious for the person confessing. In the New Testament it is written, "If we say that we have no sin, we deceive ourselves, and the truth is not in us. . . . If we say that we have not sinned, we make [God] a liar, and His word is not in us" (1 John 1:8, 10).

If this is all we can say in Confession, hard questions must be asked: How seriously do we take Jesus' call to repentance? How seriously do we take the Sacrament of Confession? How seriously did we prepare for it? It is far better to tell our priest, "I don't know what my sins are. Will you help me, Father?"

2. "I Am a Sinner"

I don't mean that we should not say this but that we shouldn't stop there. Confession must not become a ritual formality we go through to fulfill a religious obligation. It must be real and personal. When we approach Confession, we should be able to echo the words of David: "A sacrifice to God is a broken spirit, / A broken and humbled heart God will not despise" (Ps. 50:19/51:17).

3. "I've Got a Problem"

Too often, we let Confession become a counseling session in which we tell the priest our problems and hope for advice, help, or encouragement. We can and should discuss our problems with our priest, but the place for that is in his office in a special counseling session. Confession deals with sins. There is much truth in the notion that the root of every problem is sin—our own and/ or someone else's. It is our own sinfulness that underlies our problems. This is what we must unearth in our preparation and bring to Confession. The problems themselves can be addressed elsewhere.

4. *Excuses*

Excuses such as, "Sure I drink, Father, but if you knew my wife..." have no place in Confession. We come to Confession to be forgiven, not excused. C. S. Lewis explains the difference:

> Forgiveness says, "Yes, you have done this thing, but I accept your apology; I will never hold it against you and everything between us will be exactly as it was before." But excusing says, "I can see you couldn't help it or didn't mean it; you weren't really to blame." If one was not really to blame then there is nothing to forgive. . . . God knows all the real excuses very much better than we do. If there are real "extenuating circumstances" there is no fear that He will overlook them. . . . All the real excusing He will do. What we have got to do is take to Him the inexcusable bit, the sin.[6]

5. *Our Neighbors' Sins*

Excuses such as "My husband drinks too much" are out, too. We must confess *our* sins, not those of our neighbors, friends, or relatives. We may need to confess our sinful reaction to our neighbor's failings. Have we become self-righteous? Are we judging? unforgiving? Do we want revenge? Only after repenting of such sins can we begin to seek a Christian solution to the problems another's sins have created for us. These we are free to discuss with the priest at another time, of course.

6. *"I Try to Be Good"*

Priests find this one frustrating, too. It's like saying "I try not to murder anyone." The obvious response is "Have you succeeded?" It is important to remember that everyone is good—made in the

---

6 C. S. Lewis, "On Forgiveness," in *The Weight of Glory* (New York: Macmillan, 1980), 122–23.

image and likeness of God. But good people still say, do, think, and feel sinful things. Also, if you are coming to Confession, the priest assumes you are trying to be good. The question is, where are you failing?

LET'S END THIS SECTION on a positive note. There is one thing you *can* say: the same sins you confessed last time. Don't be afraid to repeat yourself confession after confession. And don't become cynical about Confession because it always seems to consist of the same old sins.

First, the Fathers teach that there are some sins and passions we will have to wrestle with for most, if not all, of our lives. And second, we can feel encouraged that we are at least holding our own. To confess one time that we covet our neighbor's goods and the next time that we have become a burglar is not spiritual progress.

We may find some comfort in a story that Metropolitan Anthony Bloom tells about the Western saint Philip Neri.

> He was an irascible man who quarreled easily and had vio-
> lent outbursts of anger and of course endured violent out-
> bursts from his brothers. One day he felt that it could not
> go on. . . . he ran to the chapel, fell down before a statue of
> Christ and begged Him to free him from his anger. He then
> walked out full of hope. The first person he met was one of
> the brothers who had never aroused the slightest anger in
> him, but for the first time in his life this brother was offen-
> sive and unpleasant to him. So Philip burst out with anger.
> . . . So Philip ran back to the chapel, cast himself before the
> statue of Christ and said, "O Lord, have I not asked you to
> free me from this anger?" And the Lord answered, "Yes,
> Philip, and for this reason I am multiplying the occasions
> for you to learn."[7]

---

7 Anthony Bloom, *Beginning to Pray* (New York: Paulist Press, 1970), 35–36.

WHAT ABOUT THE PRIEST?

For many, the greatest obstacle to confessing well, or perhaps at all, is that we must confess to a priest. This is perhaps even more frightening than what we might discover when we try see ourselves in the light of what God is calling us to be. Therefore, a few words about the priest seem appropriate.

1. The Priest's Function

The first thing we must remember is that we do not confess to the priest; we confess to Christ. Orthodox service books instruct the priest to say to the penitent, "Christ stands here invisibly and receives your confession. . . . I am only a witness." In Confession, the priest gives witness to two things: the repentance of the sinner who confesses and the forgiveness of Christ given freely to the sinner. Christ imparts this forgiveness to the penitent through the priest, to whom our Lord entrusted the ministry of forgiveness in accordance with His words, "Receive the Holy Spirit. If you forgive the sins of any, they are forgiven them; if you retain the *sins* of any, they are retained" (John 20:22–23).

The priest serves not as a judge but as witness to the reality of one's repentance. That is why, in the Orthodox practice of Confession, the priest does not face the penitent, but both priest and penitent face an icon. To show that the forgiveness comes not from the priest but from Christ, the priest does not say, "I forgive you" but, "May God forgive you."

Absolution is the concluding proclamation of repentance and forgiveness. Traditionally, it takes the form of a prayer: "May the Lord God forgive you . . ." In Slavonic service books, there is a formula that includes "I absolve you," but this is actually a later, Western addition to the prayer. It is confusing and, happily, falling into disuse.

Since absolution proclaims that the repentance is authentic, the priest is obliged to be a truthful witness and withhold absolution if: (a) there is no repentance or desire to stop an obviously sinful activity or way of life; (b) there is a failure to acknowledge a sin as being, in fact, sinful; or (c) the person is not a believer. That is, he or she does not truly accept the dogmatic and moral teachings of the Church.

The priest may also delay absolution for a time of penance. During this period, the priest may prescribe extra fasting, silence, special prayers, reading, and/or further discussions. The priest does this to help the penitent realize the true and serious nature of the sin and to deepen his or her repentance. In the case of a publicly known sin, penance may be given to avoid creating scandal for others.

The priest is also expected (though not required) to give a word of exhortation. This can include a "diagnosis," in which the priest helps the penitent uncover the causes or passions underlying the confessed sins, and a "prescription" of things the penitent should do to avoid the sin in the future, including prayers and readings to help the penitent in his or her struggle with sin.

2. What Will He Think of Me?

We all want others to like us and think well of us, and this is especially true regarding authority figures such as our priest. When a priest sees someone wrestle with their fear and embarrassment and overcome them to make an important confession, he shares in the heavenly rejoicing of which Jesus speaks: "There will be more joy in heaven over one sinner who repents than over ninety-nine just persons who need no repentance" (Luke 15:7).

Related to this is the feeling we sometimes get that our priest has used our confession in his sermon. I suspect that everyone who confesses gets this feeling from time to time. But what we may not realize is that twenty people may have confessed the same sin in the past month, that Sunday's Gospel may deal specifically with that sin, and, besides, the priest may be struggling with that sin, too.

3. Why Confess to Him? He's a Sinner!

Why go to a doctor? He gets sick, too! In fact, it should be easier to confess to another sinner. Regarding Jesus, it is written, "For in that He Himself has suffered, being tempted, He is able to aid those who are tempted" (Heb. 2:18). We can also say that a priest can use his own struggles with sin to help those who come to him. In turn, the penitent's struggle can strengthen and instruct the priest, who must also repent. One of the most loving gifts we can give a priest is a good confession.

IN CONCLUSION

The two great obstacles to confessing well are laziness and fear. Laziness prevents us from taking the time and making the effort to prepare well. Fear prevents us from being open and honest with ourselves and our God before another Christian, our priest. We should confess these sins, as well.

When we move beyond our laziness and fear, we will discover that the Father of our Lord Jesus Christ, who has become our Father as well, is very much like the father of the Prodigal Son. He stands on the high place watching for us. When He sees we have taken the smallest step to return to Him, He forgets His dignity and reserve and runs to meet us. He opens His arms to embrace us, and He takes us with Him to the place where He dwells.

An Examination of Conscience

To help you personally prepare for the Sacrament of Confession, we suggest you find time to sit quietly and prayerfully examine your life using the following examination of conscience as a guide.[8]

1. *When Jesus saw him lying there, and knew that he already had been in that condition a long time, He said to him, "Do you want to be made well? (John 5:6)*
»   What is my attitude to this confession? Have I prepared for it? Am I sincerely willing to change aspects of my life so that they will be more in keeping with the Gospel? Did I forget or hide any serious sins in my last confession? Have I made reparation to anyone I have injured? Since my last confession, have I remained firm in my efforts to change my life, or did I give up due to laziness, discouragement, or forgetfulness?

2. *Jesus said to him, "'You shall love the LORD your God with all your heart, with all your soul, and with all your mind.' This is the first and great commandment." (Matt. 22:37–38)*
»   Do I really love God above all things? Or are worldly things such as possessions, power, or popularity more important

---

8   This examination is based on those found in *The Way of the Pilgrim* (New York: Pueblo Publishing Company, 1976) and *The Rites of the Catholic Church* (Collegeville, MN: The Liturgical Press, 1976).

to me? Have I placed my trust in these or in such things as horoscopes, occult practices, or superstitions?

» Have I prayed on a regular and daily basis? Do I pray attentively? Do I approach prayer with joy and enthusiasm, or do I allow anything, no matter how trivial, to be an excuse to shorten prayer or avoid it entirely? Do I think about God during the course of my day?

3. *"Therefore whoever confesses Me before men, him I will also confess before My Father who is in heaven. But whoever denies Me before men, him I will also deny before My Father who is in heaven." (Matt. 10:32–33)*

» Am I willing to be known as a Christian in public and private life? Was I embarrassed or afraid to admit my belief in Christ and His Church to others? If someone said something unfair or inaccurate about Christ or Christianity, did I try to speak the truth with gentleness, respect, and love?

4. *Always be ready to give a defense to everyone who asks you a reason for the hope that is in you. (1 Pet. 3:15)*

» Do I know what the Orthodox Church teaches and believes? Have I taken the time to read, study, or learn more about my faith? Am I able and willing to answer questions about Christ, the Church, and my faith?

» Did I read, study, or meditate on God's Word in the Bible daily?

5. *Bring to the Lord glory and honor. / Bring to the Lord the glory due His name. (Ps. 28/29:1–2)*

» Do I keep Sundays and feast days holy by participating as fully as possible in the liturgical services? Do I observe the fasting days and seasons of the Church? Do I receive our Lord's Body and Blood in Holy Communion frequently? Did I prepare diligently for Holy Communion by prayer and fasting?

6. *[Submit] to one another in the fear of God. (Eph. 5:21)*

»   Am I faithful and loyal to my spouse? Am I honest, respect-
    ful, and kind to him or her? Am I grateful for my spouse? Do
    I honor my husband or wife in my heart, in our home, and in
    public? Do I often pray for him or her?

»   Have I honored and obeyed my parents, showing them love
    and respect and helping them with their material, emotional,
    and spiritual needs? Have I been loving, patient, and under-
    standing with my children? Did I discipline them appropri-
    ately? Have I tried to impart my faith to them by word and
    example? Do I contribute to the peace and well-being of my
    family by offering my time, service, and love?

»   In my job or profession, am I an honest and hard worker?
    Do I view the service I render my employers and others as
    service done to and for Christ? Do I pay my employees a
    fair wage? Are my expectations of them fair and reasonable?
    Have I fulfilled my promises, contracts, and obligations?

»   Have I respected and obeyed legitimate authority? Have I
    voted responsibly and knowledgeably? Have I paid my taxes?
    Do I work as I am able to promote peace, justice, morality,
    and love in my community, my country, and the world?

»   Do I use my positions of responsibility and authority for the
    good of others?

7. *Jesus said: "Love your enemies, do good to those who hate you,
    bless those who curse you, and pray for those who spitefully use
    you. To him who strikes you on the one cheek, offer the other
    also. And from him who takes away your cloak, do not with-
    hold your tunic either." (Luke 6:27–29)*

»   Have I caused injury to another's life, health, spiritual or
    emotional well-being, or material possessions by violence or
    neglect?

»   Have I advised or helped someone to obtain an abortion?

»   Have I quarreled, been unduly angry with, or insulted
    anyone? Have I reconciled with them? If I have injured or

offended anyone, have I sought their forgiveness? If anyone
has injured or offended me, have I forgiven them? Or am I
still filled with hatred or a desire for revenge?

» Am I committed to accepting suffering rather than
inflicting it?
» Did I seek to retaliate in the face of provocation or violence
of any sort?
» Do I strive for peace within myself and work to be a peace-
maker in my daily life?

8. *For this is the will of God, your sanctification: that you should
abstain from sexual immorality; that each of you should know
how to possess his own vessel in sanctification and honor,
not in passion of lust like the Gentiles who do not know God.
(1 Thess. 4:3–5)*

» Have I been faithful to my spouse?
» Have I exercised self-control in regard to food, drink, drugs,
and sexual desire? Have I misused my sexuality by fornica-
tion, masturbation, impure thoughts, or fantasies? Have I
participated in indecent conversations or used pornography?
» Have I incited others to sin by my own failures in this area?

9. *Jesus said: "Take heed and beware of covetousness, for one's life
does not consist in the abundance of the things he possesses."
(Luke 12:15)*

» Have I envied or desired inordinately another's position or
property? Have I stolen or damaged the property of others?
Did I restore it or make restitution?
» Do I share my possessions with those who have less? Do I
give freely and generously of my time, talent, and money to
those in need and/or the church?

10. *If anyone among you thinks he is religious, and does not bridle
his tongue but deceives his own heart, this one's religion is use-
less. (James 1:26)*

» Have I taken the name of the Lord in vain? Have I blasphemed or used profane language?

» Do I talk too much and listen too little?

» Have I lied or, by cowardly silence, avoided telling the truth? Have I gossiped or spread rumors about others? Have I spoken harshly, unjustly, unnecessarily, or insultingly to anyone or about anyone?

» Do I spend time in silence? Or must I always be talking or have music or the television on?

» Have I been boastful about myself or judgmental of others?

11. *Whatever you do, do all to the glory of God. (1 Cor. 10:31)*

» Am I motivated first and foremost by a desire to love and serve God and my neighbor in the way God wills me to?

» Do I think of myself as better than others?

» When I pray, fast, or do any good, do I try to do it secretly? Or, by word or display, do I make sure that others notice me and my works?

12. *Cast your care upon the Lord, / And He shall support you; / He will never allow the righteous to be moved. (Ps. 54:23/55:22)*

» Am I anxious or worried about anything? Is there a problem or hurt that I should bring to the Lord in Confession for forgiveness, healing, or guidance?

Appendix

QUOTES FROM THE FATHERS

Saint John Chrysostom on Repentance

No sin is so great that it can conquer the munificence of the Master. Even if one is a fornicator, or an adulterer . . . the power of the gift and the love of the Master are great enough to make all these sins disappear and to make the sinner shine more brightly than the rays of the sun.

And Christ Himself, addressing the whole human race, said: "Come to me, all you who labor and are burdened, and I will give you rest."

His invitation is one of kindness, His goodness is beyond description.

And see whom He calls! Those who have spent their strength in breaking the law, those who are burdened with their sins, those who can no longer lift up their heads, those who are filled with shame, those who can no longer speak out. And why does He call them? Not to demand an accounting, nor to hold court. But why? To relieve them of their pain, to take away their heavy burden. For what could ever be a heavier burden than sin? . . . I shall refresh you who are weighted down by sin, He says, and you who are bent down as if under a burden; I shall grant you remission of your sins. Only come to Me!

Saint Isaac of Syria on Repentance

Repentance (*metanoia*) is fitting at all times and for all persons, for sinners as well as for the righteous who look for salvation. There are no bounds to perfection, for even the perfection of the most perfect is nothing but imperfection. Hence, until the moment of death, neither the time nor the works of perfection can ever be complete.

Saint John of Karpathos on Repentance

Do all in your power not to fall, for the strong athlete should not fall. But if you do fall, get up again at once and continue the contest. Even if you fall a thousand times . . . rise up again each time, and keep on doing this until the day of your death. For it is written, "If a righteous man falls seven times," that is, repeatedly throughout his life, seven times shall he rise again."

Saint John Climacus on God's Mercy

It is the property of angels not to fall, and even, as some say, it is quite impossible for them to fall. It is the property of men to fall, and to rise again as often as this may happen. But it is the property of devils, and devils alone, not to rise once they have fallen.

PSALMS OF REPENTANCE[9]

Psalm 6/7

O Lord, rebuke me not in Your anger nor chasten me in Your wrath.

Have mercy on me, O Lord, for I am weak; heal me, for my bones are troubled.

My soul also is sorely troubled. But You, O Lord—how long?

Turn, O Lord, save my life; deliver me for the sake of Your mercy.

For in death there is no remembrance of You; in Sheol who can give You praise?

I am weary with my moaning; every night I flood my bed with tears; I drench my couch with my weeping.

My eye wastes away because of grief; it grows weak because of all my foes.

Depart from me, all you workers of evil; for the Lord has heard the sound of my weeping.

The Lord has heard my supplication; the Lord accepts my prayer.

All my enemies shall be ashamed and sorely troubled; they shall turn back and be put to shame in a moment.

Psalm 31/32

Blessed is he whose transgression is forgiven, whose sin is covered.

Blessed is the man to whom the Lord imputes no iniquity and in whose mouth there is no deceit.

When I declared not my sin, my body wasted away through my groaning all day long.

For day and night Your hand was heavy upon me; my strength was dried up as by the heat of summer.

I acknowledged my sin to You, and I did not hide my iniquity.

---

9 Psalms are taken from *The Ancient Faith Psalter* (Chesterton, IN: Ancient Faith Publishing, 2016).

I said, "I will confess my transgressions to the Lord"; then You
forgave the ungodliness of my heart.

For his sin, everyone who is godly will offer prayer to You at a
fitting time; and the rush of great waters shall not reach him.

You are my hiding place from the affliction that surrounds me;
my joy, to deliver me from those who encompass me.

"I will instruct you and teach you the way you should go; I will
set my eyes upon you."

Be not like a horse or a mule, without understanding, which
must be curbed with bit and bridle, or else it will not keep
with you.

Many are the pangs of the wicked; but mercy surrounds him
who trusts in the Lord.

Be glad in the Lord and rejoice, O righteous, and shout for joy, all
you upright in heart!

Psalm 37/38

O Lord, rebuke me not in Your anger, nor chasten me in Your
wrath.

For Your arrows have sunk into me, and Your hand has come
down on me.

There is no soundness in my flesh because of Your indignation;
there is no health in my bones because of my sins.

For my iniquities have gone over my head; they weigh like a burden too heavy for me.

My wounds grow foul and fester because of my foolishness; I
am utterly bowed down and prostrate; all the day I go about
mourning.

For my soul is filled with burning, and there is no soundness in
my flesh.

I am utterly spent and crushed; I groan because of the tumult of
my heart.

O Lord, all my longing is known to You; my sighing is not hidden from You.

My heart throbs, my strength fails me, and the light of my eyes—
it also has gone from me.
My friends and companions stand aloof from my plague, and my
kinsmen stand afar off.
Those who seek my life lay their snares; those who seek my hurt
speak of ruin and meditate treachery all the day long.
But I am like a deaf man; I do not hear, like a dumb man who
does not open his mouth.
I am like a man who does not hear and in whose mouth are no
rebukes.
But in You, O Lord, have I hoped; You, O Lord my God, will
answer.
For I pray, "Only let them not rejoice over me," who boast against
me when my foot slips.
For I am ready to fall, and my pain is ever with me. I confess my
iniquity; I am sorry for my sin.
But those who are my foes without cause are mighty, and many
are those who hate me wrongfully.
Those who render me evil for good are my adversaries, because I
follow after good.
Do not forsake me, O Lord! O my God, be not far from me!
Make haste to help me, O Lord, my salvation!

Psalm 50/51

Have mercy on me, O God, according to Your steadfast love;
according to your abundant mercy, blot out my transgressions.
Wash me thoroughly from my iniquity and cleanse me from
my sin.
For I know my transgressions, and my sin is ever before me.
Against You, You only, have I sinned and done that which is evil
in Your sight,
so that You are justified in Your sentence and blameless in Your
judgment.

Behold, I was brought forth in iniquity, and in sin did my mother conceive me.

Behold, You desire truth in the inward being; therefore, teach me wisdom in my secret heart.

Purge me with hyssop, and I shall be clean; wash me, and I shall be whiter than snow.

Fill me with joy and gladness; let the bones which You have broken rejoice.

Hide Your Face from my sins and blot out all my iniquities.

Create in me a clean heart, O God, and put a new and right spirit within me.

Cast me not away from Your presence, and take not Your Holy Spirit from me.

Restore to me the joy of Your salvation, and uphold me with a willing spirit.

Then I will teach transgressors Your ways, and sinners will return to You.

Deliver me from bloodguilt, O God, God of my salvation, and my tongue will sing aloud of Your deliverance.

O Lord, open my lips, and my mouth shall show forth Your praise.

For You have no delight in sacrifice; were I to give a burnt offering, You would not be pleased.

The sacrifice acceptable to God is a broken spirit; a broken and contrite heart, O God, You will not despise.

Do good to Zion in Your good pleasure; rebuild the walls of Jerusalem;

then will You delight in right sacrifices, in burnt offerings and whole burnt offerings; then bulls will be offered on Your altar.

Psalm 101/102

Hear my prayer, O Lord; let my cry come to You!
Do not turn Your Face from me in the day of my distress!
Incline Your ear to me; hear me speedily in the day when I call!

For my days have vanished like smoke, and my bones have been parched like a stick.

I am blighted like grass, and my heart is withered, for I have forgotten to eat my bread.

Because of my loud groaning, my bones cleave to my flesh.

I have become like a pelican of the wilderness, like an owl in a ruined house.

I have watched and have become like a lonely sparrow on the housetop.

All the day my enemies taunt me; those who praised me have sworn against me.

For I have eaten ashes like bread and mingle tears with my drink because of Your indignation and anger; for You have taken me up and thrown me away.

My days have declined like a shadow; I wither away like grass.

But You, O Lord, endure forever; Your memory is from generation to generation.

You will arise and have mercy on Zion; it is time to have mercy on her; the time has come.

For Your servants hold her stones dear and have pity on her dust.

The nations will fear the name of the Lord, and all the kings of the earth Your glory.

For the Lord will build up Zion; He will appear in His glory; He has regarded the prayer of the humble and has not despised their supplication.

Let this be recorded for a generation to come, so that a people yet uncreated shall praise the Lord:

for He has looked down from His holy height; from heaven the Lord looked at the earth

to hear the groans of the prisoners, to set free the sons of those who were slain,

to declare the name of the Lord in Zion, and in Jerusalem His praise,

when peoples gather together, and kings, to serve the Lord.

Man asked the Lord in the course of his strength, "Make me to know the shortness of my days."

Take me not away in the midst of my days: Your years endure throughout all generations!

You, O Lord, in the beginning laid the foundation of the earth, and the heavens are the work of Your hands.

They will perish, but You remain; and they will all grow old like a garment; like a cloak You will fold them up, and they will be changed.

But You are the same, and Your years will not fail.

The children of Your servants shall dwell securely; their seed shall be led forever in the way of righteousness.

Psalm 129/130

Out of the depths I cry to You, O Lord. Lord, hear my voice.

Let Your ears be attentive to the voice of my supplication.

If You, O Lord, should mark iniquities, Lord, who could stand?

But there is forgiveness with You, that You may be feared.

For Your name's sake I have waited for You, O Lord; my soul has hoped on the Lord.

From the morning watch until night,
     from the morning watch, let Israel hope on the Lord.

For with the Lord there is steadfast love, and with Him is plenteous redemption,

and He will deliver Israel from all his iniquities.

Psalm 142/143

Hear my prayer, O Lord; give ear to my supplications! In Your faithfulness answer me, in Your righteousness!

Enter not into judgment with Your servant; for no man living is righteous before You.

For the enemy has pursued me; he has crushed my life to the ground; he has made me sit in darkness like those long dead.

Therefore my spirit faints within me; my heart within me is appalled.

I remember the days of old; I meditate on all that You have done; I muse on what Your hands have wrought.

I stretch out my hands to You; my soul thirsts for You like a parched land.

Make haste to answer me, O Lord! My spirit fails!

Hide not Your Face from me, lest I be like those who go down to the Pit.

Let me hear in the morning of Your steadfast love, for in You I put my trust.

Teach me the way I should go, for to You I lift up my soul.

Deliver me, O Lord, from my enemies! I have fled to You for refuge!

Teach me to do Your will, for You are my God.

Let Your good Spirit lead me on a level path.

For Your name's sake, O Lord, preserve my life. In Your righteousness bring me out of trouble.

And in Your steadfast love cut off my enemies and destroy all my adversaries, for I am Your servant.

We hope you have enjoyed and benefited from this book. Your financial support makes it possible to continue our nonprofit ministry both in print and online. Because the proceeds from our book sales only partially cover the costs of operating **Ancient Faith Publishing** and **Ancient Faith Radio**, we greatly appreciate the generosity of our readers and listeners. Donations are tax deductible and can be made at **www.ancientfaith.com.**

To view our other publications,
please visit our website: **store.ancientfaith.com**

 ANCIENT FAITH RADIO

Bringing you Orthodox Christian music, readings, prayers, teaching, and podcasts 24 hours a day since 2004 at **www.ancientfaith.com**

www.ingramcontent.com/pod-product-compliance
Lightning Source LLC
Chambersburg PA
CBHW031300120626
46545CB00007B/2905